Art is an attitude
toward life. If you aim
your work and your life high,
keep your scene harmonious, then
you're an artist and your life a
art.

— Gage Taylor

'03
Stephanie Davis

A Poet's Poetic Expressions

Mustard Seeds

Joseph Seymour Jones

VANTAGE PRESS
New York

To my mother for her faith
during some very difficult times

FIRST EDITION

Published by Vantage Press, Inc.
516 West 34th Street, New York, New York 10001

Manufactured in the United States of America
ISBN: 0-533-13652-0

Library of Congress Catalog Card No.: 00-92155

0 9 8 7 6 5 4 3 2

Indexed Table of Poems

Introduction vii

A Millennium's Reflection Is a Future's Mirror 4
A Pattern for World Peace 1
A Poet's President 46
A Tender Heart Can Be Healed 29
A Virtuous Woman 80
Am I Human or Animal?. 87
Are Teachers Really Born or Made? 83
Behavior Can Be Improved 63
Blueprint for a Good Life 84
Children of Prediction—Born to Circumstance 28
Close, Cold Blood, Jesus! 12
Criticizing Teachers 82
Desire to Carry On 38
Destimated and Know It. 85
Dichotomy of America. 50
Did You Ever Want To? 67
Every Day Is Sent From Above 11
Everyday Frustrations—Simplified in Prayer 79
Favor for Me 37
Footsteps of a True Servant 27
For a Niece as You Marry. 39
Foundations for Building 59
God's Love Comes Through 14
His Second Coming. 9
I Know a King!. 22
I Once Befriended a Tree 69
I Set Goals 26
In Loving Memory of Jerome Fitzgerald Jones. 31
Instruments of Productivity. 61
It's Not the World But the People in It 71
Judgments of Worth 56
Lady! The World Forever Thanks You! 24

Life's Sentence to Nine Numbers.................... 88
Mother 42
Mother's Cry 44
Motive Can Be Rationalized........................ 16
Mustard-Seed Rewards............................. 55
My True Friend Passed Away Today................. 35
Our World Today................................... 15
Pages of History 76
Peace on Earth 17
People Are Like Pillars............................ 73
People Really Do Matter! 72
Picking Up My Shade 68
Pleading True to the Games........................ 64
Prosperity 20
Rain for No Simple Reason......................... 19
Resting in the Loving Arms of Jesus................ 81
Self-esteem or Destimation 21
Sorry for the Delay 53
Spirited Souls Are Free........................... 60
Test Time Is Stress Time 65
Thanks for Your Kindness 43
The Best of Times 6
The "Business Lady"............................... 49
The Diligent Postal Worker 45
The Gift of Opportunity 23
The Greatest Grandfather 33
The Ultimate of All Providers 52
This Woman We Call "Grace"........................ 47
Thugs 66
Time Belongs...................................... 62
To Earn One's Own True Freedom 86
To Heal a Broken Spirit 58
To Incriminate the People 77
To Inspire True Democratic Ideals 78
To Invest in Another's Downfall 75
To Lead a True Democracy! 13
To Think About Community......................... 74

Transaction Benders. 57
Tribute to a Great Sister 41
Tribute to a Legend: "Big Jim" Jones 30
Until We Meet Again 34
Upon Your Birth 51
Visions of Peace. 3
When a Dark Cloud Gets Darker. 54

Introduction

These poetic expressions center themselves around topics and subjects written from many very diverse experiences and interests. Some of these expressions were requested by individuals who interceded for others who often needed words that inspire visual images of some of the truths in the genuineness of their hearts.

Many of the other poetic expressions are the results of some other spiritual voices of intercession resulting from an inherent need to create printed forms to appreciate for what they came to be.

I bear an eternal debt to my mother, Mrs. "Big Jim" (Sallie Carstarphen) Jones, for her suggestion one Sunday morning that I send the only scripted poem in my written possession to a poetry outlet during one of their open poetry contests. Since that January 1998 date, I became grounded on a course that has changed my life forever.

To Mary's Little Baby Jesus and God His Father, be all the glory!

A Pattern for World Peace
(Added to World's Largest Poem for Peace)

The world we all live in today
is in such dire need for peace
there should be—
a crying out for harmony
that leaves no soul at ease.

The cry should grow ever louder
as more senseless blood is shed
over God-designed differences
that should cause greater love instead.

But the children suffer more often
and many are not led unto God;
instead they are taught human destinies
with no belief in the strength of the rod.

But we all must remember
that a true One came along
and left the perfect pattern
for us all to carry on.

The pattern requires a faith
in many things unseen
and a belief in their fulfillment
by what the Designer has said and means.

So each of us must take our parts
and journey unto the end
as we build this world
as a place of peace
until the Designer returns again!

(August 9, 1998)

Visions of Peace
(Added to World's Largest Poem for Peace)

During difficult times,
it just seems,
that peace fades with the distance
and to let peace "fade"
means to question hope
or not have "hope"
at that very instance!

Peace must truly be a vision
communicated in a number of ways
that increases all understanding
to survive the most difficult of days!

So let's all focus
our minds and efforts
on promoting true visions of peace
whereby the brotherhood of humanity
can succeed at taming the beasts!

(August 24, 1999)

A Millennium's Reflection Is a Future's Mirror

A millennium's reflection
is a future's mirror
where one thousand years have passed
and what lies ahead
for one thousand years
is another period of time
that will last!

A millennium's reflection
is a future's mirror
of what reality will bring into being
as the reign of Christ
over God's creation
shall be worthy
of witnessing and seeing!

A millennium's reflection
is a future's mirror
where so much has already been achieved
and all that remains
is the great confirmation
that Christ shall truly be believed!

In a millennium's reflection
as a future's mirror,
many prophecies
shall have already been fulfilled
as all of God's discipled children
shall answer His call and will!

So reflect on a millennium
as a future's mirror
and be glad to finally know the truths
as all human knowledge
and great understanding
shall be fortified
in the strength of youth!

(January 1, 2000)

The Best of Times

Recalling the best of times
over the courses of history
requires reflections upon the simpleness
of how things used to be!

In the stone age times seemed hard
and more patience was required
to gain the bare necessities
and reach goals that were desired!

During the era of the pharaohs
bondage appeared to dominate
the lives of those held captive
over the faith they would demonstrate!

When faith had moved mountains
and better times had come along,
the era of humane rebirth
made the weak appear very strong!

With time came exploration
and the desire to go beyond
the truths that had been given
over choices to not respond!

In the age of inventive discovery
much was made to appear new
as knowledge advanced understanding
and the dominance of humanity grew!

In the times of great expansion
many territories became the "claimed"
and those left to the wilderness
never remained the same!

Where titles did not exist
nothing really seemed to matter
because disputes could linger on
and war would make it no better!

Between natural resources and those man-made
time would bring conservation
through the era of "want" and "want" not
in the growth of many nations!

With efforts to strike a balance
so-called "depressions" came along
and tested many ethical policies
for a correct balance to carry on!

But with the modern age of advances
many have failed to see
the relationships between the masses
and the outcomes for humanity!

For many choices have been made
and decisions to not accept
that resources are actually limited
and unnecessary consumption can be helped!

By establishing appropriate priorities
and staying committed to basic goals,
many benefits can be realized
to help the nations as a whole!

Since time has entered an era
where strife has hurt the spirit
and left little or no room for error
for the inevitable or reasons to fear it!

Now all people must assume their roles
in understanding the depths of history
and take their places consciously
while accepting life's mysteries!

(February 3, 2000)

His Second Coming

When Jesus came the first time,
He spent that time quite well.
He took great advantage of every moment
to save all His souls from Hell!

He cleansed the sins
of each of us,
even before going on to the cross
and "wrote" the pattern
for all to follow
with Him as author and boss!

He spoke of His Second Coming,
which His true believers
know is true
because His word has everything
each believer needs
to make it through!

And within His Second Coming,
all things will be fulfilled
as all God's "discipled" children
shall answer His call and will!

So watch the air
and things everywhere
as signs and wonders appear
and know faithfully
in your heart and mind

that His Second Coming is drawing near!

(Titled & Requested By Mr. Wayne Brock)
(September 30, 1999)

Every Day Is Sent From Above

In the morning when I rise,
I will give God thanks
when I open my eyes!

Every day is sent from above!

And as I face the rising sun,
I will give God thanks
for all that He's done!

Every day is sent from above!

Jesus, I love you!

And will forever be true to you!
You came into my life
and made my living just fine!

Every day is sent from above!
Every day is sent from above!

(1978)

Close, Cold Blood, Jesus!

In a prayer of urgency!
Lord, I come to thee!
Close, cold blood, Jesus!

Something suddenly manifested
I never thought I would see!
Close, cold blood, Jesus!

A spirit suddenly burdened
by the spirit of a projected judge
quickening the pleas for mercy
as orders and decrees are adjudged!

Close, cold blood, Jesus!

(August 30, 1998)

To Lead a True Democracy!

To lead a true democracy
requires a guidance from above
and a spiritual walk
with a humble heart
as gentle as a dove!

To lead a true democracy
requires a most special touch
with diplomatic doctrines
and integrity that means so much!

To lead a true democracy
requires a commitment to harmony
and a respect for all priorities
that promote domestic tranquility!

To lead a true democracy
requires a vision that parallels
the courses of actions
that are necessary
so that true democracy can prevail!

(August 30, 1998)

13

God's Love Comes Through

*Times will seem hard
but go on through anyway
and no matter how hard things get,
take the time to pray!*

*And don't be rushed to judge
God's blessed souls
and find yourself against
a God who is strong and bold!*

*Always be temperate
and sincere in all you do
and you will always see
the love of God coming through!*

(1998)

Our World Today

*Our world today seems challenged
and there's so much going on.
We can look all around us
and find the things that's wrong!*

*Many fail to receive the message
with confusion taking over today.
This is why we must offer hope
in the things we do and say!*

(1998)

Motive Can Be Rationalized

Motive can be something strange
as to what others will or will not try.
It cannot always be determined
as some conclusion to judge others by!

But to look as motive as reason
means to rationalize one's motivation
and take a closer look at things
that can govern most situations!

(June 11, 1999)

Peace on Earth

Once upon a time
not long ago,
I saw the stars above
and the moon aglow!

This sight unseen,
this many splendid thing
from the here and now
spoke words untold
of the ages old!

What great creation
this universe;
what awesome wonders
we find on earth!

Timeless eternity,
endless as the gifts we see!

But as the days go by,
we see children cry!

As the hearts of man
turns to stone again!

While we fail to see
Truth in reality!

Or work to build bridges
—of hope
—of love
—of peace on earth!

(1999)

Rain for No Simple Reason

*The sun was so beautiful and bright today
amid a cloudless sky of blue, not gray!*

*As I felt warmth of the sun's soft rays,
I tried to imagine it
lasting for day after day!*

*But in reality we need the sun and rain
working in harmony
to help make nature to change!*

*In season out of season
rain for no simple reason!
Sunshine friend of mine
in season, out of season!*

(1998)

Prosperity

It's not the will of man
that God's children should prosper
nor must consent be given
to the things on God's roster!

To criticize God's will in discontent
is to solidify one's own very end
because man's will is not God's will
and He rules with a very strong hand!

So be conscious of words, deeds, and actions,
as God knows each and every heart
and through His most divine will
the world shall know "How Great Thou Art!"

(September 8, 1999)

Self-esteem or Destimation

What is it to build self-esteem?
Is this a process that one goes through
or is there some other opposite
that others try to build up in you!

Destimation may be that other opposite—
a process where self-esteem is torn down
and what is left or substituted
is not a smile but a frown!

(May 25, 1998)

21

I Know a King!

Christ is the infinite example
of the true Prince of Peace
who faced the ultimate
subjectivizating challenges
of any world principality!

This fact alone solidifies
all knowledge, understanding and conclusions

Because I know a King:

His crown was made of thorns;
His emblem is the cross;
and His power is His blood!

(1990 and 1999)

The Gift of Opportunity
(Spring Hill College)

Many gifts have virtue as value
far beyond real or true measure
because each gift represents an investment
into the future we will someday treasure!

The treasure is multiplied over humanity
as, one by one, others become a part
of the wealth of the human potential
rooted in the strength
of a seed's early start!

So as each of us embrace the future
accepting the known and unknown to be,
let us multiply the value of each other
as we support lives through opportunity!

(February 2, 1999)

Lady! The World Forever Thanks You!
(Tribute to Princess Diana)

You were brought up in a way
that anyone should aspire to be
with compassion for less fortunate ones
and respect for humanity.

Your life mirrored great virtues
that have graced eternity
leaving footprints on the sands of time
for what is or is to be.

Lady! The world forever thanks you!
And will forever cherish your memory!
For all that you were;
ever hoped for or dreamed;
or did forever aspire to be!

For what titles could not give
to the spirit of the will
helped to mean much more than reality.

It's with regret and gratitude
that we bid farewell to you;
you lived to do all you could do
and the best always came through.

You left no shame of kindness
as you lived your life;
you were as kind as you could be;
a special gift from heaven;
a precious soul,
sent to help make others free.

That's why your strength and dignity
are etched in your memory
like the love you gave
to this world in need.

And it's forever and always
that we look to a brighter day
and keep the memory of you,
You wonderful Lady!

Lady! The world forever thanks you!
And will forever cherish your memory!
For all that you were;
ever hoped for or dreamed;
or did forever aspire to be!

(September 6, 1997)

I Set Goals
(In Memory of Jerome Fitzgerald Jones)

I set goals and work hard to achieve;
I know no goal is out of reach
when I am willing to believe.

The sky can be the limit
to the good that I can do;
but I must work unceasingly
to make my dreams come true.

Some people will believe in me
and support the good I do;
others will be discouraging
and say, "Dreams don't come true!"

That is why I must realize
I am the captain of my fate!
I can realize my own dreams
when I work hard and not wait.

Or give up and say,
"It can never be done!
I'll set with the setting sun!"
Only to start dreaming all over again
of all the good things
I could have done!

(May 1, 1998)

Footsteps of a True Servant
(Tribute to Mother Teresa)

The footsteps of a true servant
are not ordained but ordered instead
like the works a true servant performs
through wonders that miracles have bred!

The footsteps of a true servant
will go places that few ever go,
reaching heights in each of their callings
and reaching depths that few ever know!

The footsteps of a true servant
are guided unto their very end
by a source so great and mighty;
it's the true servant's only true friend!

As long as a true servant's footsteps
are guided by the true source above,
the results of a true servant's footsteps
will be self-sacrifice and true love!

As for the footsteps of Mother Teresa,
history will always behold
a place for her earnest-entreaty
symbolized by hands of pure gold!

(October 6, 1998)

Children of Prediction—Born to Circumstance
(Tribute to John Fitzgerald Kennedy, Jr.)

Some things are left to prediction
though unpredicted in time or space
where events unfold to destiny
that increases the need for grace!

Such are the circumstances
for those who are born unto the "son"
who prepares themselves
for an inevitable fate
that many would choose to shun!

So to truly live a full life
means to explore beyond the measure
and capture everything that is good
to place in life's greatest treasure!

(Requested on Behalf of Mrs. Jacqueline B. Kennedy
Onassis For Her Strength in Raising Two Great People)

(July 18, 1999)

A Tender Heart Can Be Healed
(For The Kennedy & Bessette Families)

*A tender heart can be healed
though the pains can seem so great
by thanking God for all His mercies
to bear what others could not take!*

*So be of good cheer
although your heart is hurt
and you may feel you are all alone;
just keep stealing away to the quiet places
where you find the strength to carry on!*

*And remember you are still
a symbol of strength
that we are all still depending on
to stand strong just as others have done
with faith to face the unknown!*

(July 22, 1999)

29

Tribute to a Legend: "Big Jim" Jones
(In Memory of Jimmie Hugh Jones, Sr.)

You left a great legacy
for us all to recall
of some "grand" times shared
and great fun had by all!

You saw no limits
to the good that you could do;
even if times seemed hard—
you proved yourself to be true!

A man who traveled many miles each day
to sign on "live"
on three different airways!

You hold records for being a first
placing Gadsden, Alabama, on the map
during an era of rebirth!

As your "base city" of Gadsden
took a look back in time
to recapture a "grand" era
that now reflects in our minds!

It is befitting to you
that your loved ones respond
with a sincere "Thank You!"
for what Gadsden has done!

(July 10, 1999)

In Loving Memory of Jerome Fitzgerald Jones

(January 31, 1961—September 16, 1978)

At the Tenth Year We Reflected:

*Since your passing we all have had
to reach deeper inside ourselves
for more of what it takes to cope,
and face a renewed determination
to pray for a better tomorrow.
At the Fifteenth Year We Reflected:*

*The fifteen years since you left us
still leaves us believing—
If the choice had been ours,
you would have stayed here
for an eternity.*

*Since the choice was not ours
and your work on earth was done,
God decided to give you
eternal rest with Him.
And Now at the Twentieth Year We Reflect That:*

We Better Understand

*We better understand these days
that challenges come in many ways.
You faced them with such grace and ease
as if you had only God to please!*

You believed all things
would work out fine;
we still hold this thought
within our minds.
You stood the tests of great humility
to endure to the end
with a soul set free!

You now abide
with heaven's peace and rest
with angels of mercy
and all of God's best.
You did leave a legacy
for others to recall
in our memories
of when you cared for us all!

Sadly missed by mother, brothers, close relatives, and
dearest friends.

(September 16, 1988, 1993, and 1998)

The Greatest Grandfather
(Tribute to Mr. Chester Hugh Jones)

With the kindness of a gentle breeze,
you captured the word gentleman with such ease
by the way you lived your life and cared,
by the way you worked, gave and shared!

Yours is a solemn kind of reward
earned through things that came real hard,
but like the soft words you would often speak
when you would "bear" it
and turn the other cheek!

Greater now are the deeds you receive
because of your strength
and the way you believed:
to make your journey now
is not even a bother
because you were the greatest grandfather!

(December 9, 1995)

Until We Meet Again
(Tribute to Aunt Nora Lee Jones)

Your work on earth is done.
You have witnessed the setting sun.
You have heard God's welcome voice.
You have heard Him say "Well Done!"

We're glad you came this way.
You gave the world your best.
Your journey has come to its end,
So Aunt Nora Lee, Rest in Peace
Until we meet again!

(September 10, 1995)

My True Friend Passed Away Today

You left us today
even though we had—
some gentle words to say!

There were some nice things,
as well, we really wanted to do
just to let you know
how much we cared for you!

Things won't be the same
without your soft voice around,
guiding us along life's journey
and picking us up
when we are down!

But for all we could not say
or for all we could not do,
one thing goes without saying—
you knew how much we loved you!

Your torchlight will be missed here—
as reality starts to set in,
but we'll thank God more and more
because we had you as a true friend!

You will be missed,
but NEVER forgotten!

(For My True Friend, Mrs. Mildred Hammac)

(June 12, 1998)

Favor for Me

You are losing your sight—
and some day you may not see;
There's one favor I'd like—
would you do it for me?

Look very close
at the things around you—
please do it while you now see;
And write pictures
when I'm old and gray—
from your strength and memory!

For then I will be the one in need
of the great teacher who has taught
Life's lessons through experience
from what life's circumstance had brought.

So please lose no time as the days pass by—
please do one favor for me!

Look very close
at the things around you—please do it while you now
see;
And write pictures
when I'm old and gray—
from your strength and memory!

(May 6, 1998)

Desire to Carry On
(For the Afflicted)

The tasks before me appear so great
I dare to support each cause
but to think of all that I can do
with my strength in just one pause!

I am but one among the many
who have trod upon threads of grace
and humbled themselves
for a daily challenge
to rise above the lowest of a place!

But for some among the many
the challenge is more than they can meet,
for they face the close
of each passing day
with a desire
to stand strong upon their feet!

So in strength there are no "forgranteds"
and when weak one truly can be strong
By their grasps that exceeds their reaches
in their desire to simply carry on!

(November 30, 1998)

For a Niece as You Marry

As a niece getting married
at a special time to be;
a bride who has waited
as a branch from a very strong tree!

In matrimony there are virtues
that have graced eternity
and you reflect those virtues
with your strength and dignity!

So hold fast to God's promises
as gifts from His eternal love
and place Him in all you do
with great reverence to Him above!

And there's no doubt
that yours shall be
blessed with so much favor
as in the vows that you exchange
in a Holy Union that you shall savor!

As your uncle I am as proud
as any uncle could ever be
just knowing that God has blessed us
to be branches from the same tree!

Since yours shall reign eternal
and your gifts shall be ordained
in Heaven's greatest fortress
as your wedding bells shall ring!
(Upon Mario Deshawn Johnson's Betrothal to Shana
Shernika)

(December 18, 1999)

Tribute to a Great Sister
(Mrs. Ruth L. Black Thames)

Though life deals us "hands"
we have no choice but to keep
you managed to move past limits
with a constant shuffle of the feet!

Through your continued dedication
and care for those you love,
you have placed the largest jewels
in your crown that awaits above!

But for simple ways to thank you
we are limited beyond measure;
that is why I made a simple request
for some inspiring words to treasure!

As you celebrate
fifty years of matrimony,
be of joy and appreciation, too
because so many have been inspired
by the obstacles
you brought them through!

(Requested by Mrs. Ollie Black Kiel on Behalf of a Great
Sister)

(May 25, 1999)

Mother

M is for the Marvelous lady
that you are
O is for the Others you care
so dearly for
T is for the Tender heart
of your very soul
H is for your Healing power
that's as good as gold
E is for your Eagerness
to help those in need
R is for your Richness
that's truly rich indeed.

(May, 1998)

Thanks for Your Kindness

Thanks for the smiles
from life's simple pleasures
and bonds of spirituality
that go beyond measure!

Thanks for your words
of great inspiration
like your respect for God
and His awesome of creations!

Thanks for your deeds
of humane sincerity
like the gifts of kindness
that you have shown to me!

(February 5, 1999)

Mother's Cry

You say to me,
"Why ask why?
Is it just because,
I made your mother cry?"

I say, "Yes!
She's cried more than enough!
Is this what you do
just to show you are tough?"

You say, "No!
I don't need any more tears!
I've done this long enough
to last for many years."

I say, "We've struggled
simply to rebuild;
to trade no good for evil
so that evil is what we yield!"

You say, "Good!
The struggles do not matter;
As long as things don't change
or even get any better!"

I say, "Remember!"
"We reap just what we sow!
I hope you respect this message
enough to let it show!"

(December 9, 1998)

44

The Diligent Postal Worker

The diligent postal worker
works with speed as a matter of time
and in many concerted efforts
puts bundles of mail behind!

The diligent postal worker
is as sincere as one can be
with a conscious for genuine effort
and a respect for humanity!

The diligent postal worker
will retire with a sense and feel
that the good that they have done
makes their contribution,
forever, more real!

(December 3, 1998)

A Poet's President

A poet's "president" is a promoter
and a visionary who truly cares
about the things that really do matter
and the mediums
through which one can share!

A poet's "president" is a believer
and has a great faith in one and all
who takes their turn
to "shine" in the spotlight
because they heard and answered the call!

A poet's "president" is an inspiration
appreciated for the good that they do
in multiplying the genuine goodness of others
with opportunities to make dreams come true!

(September 7, 1999)

This Woman We Call "Grace"

To encompass the depths of history
where an evolution has taken place
means to understand the mysteries
of this woman we call Grace!

She does not discriminate
when kinships come to call,
placing her in a "Chief's" position
to accept us one and all!

So to understand where we stand
in the worlds of histories
means to appreciate the closeness
that Grace has to you and me!

That in itself concludes the mystery
where time could really never tell
as much need not be spoken
because "truth-in-action"
is just as well!

So tokens of appreciation are due
though material ones do not matter
as much as the human tokens
that we all reach out to gather!

So accept these words as appreciation
and as thanks for just being there,
but most of all this is a thank-you
for your taking the time to simply care!

(With Forever Debt to Ms. Grace Willis for Truth &
Inspiration)

(December 8, 1999)

The "Business Lady"

The "Business Lady" is a special person
who knows just what to do and say;
she attends the tasks
of customer satisfaction
and she does it in a special kind of way!

Come rain or shine, snow or sleet,
no matter what the day of the week!

She makes her presence quite well known
by her desire to simply carry on!

So all who have known the "Business Lady"
know and appreciate her quite well
because the principles of the "Business Lady"
go beyond words that one could ever tell!

(For Miss Betty, The "Business Lady")

(February 12, 1999)

Dichotomy of America

There are many faces of a country
that goes past the dark or the light
with on one hand having a destiny
and on the other hand having foresight!

With destiny there are few choices
but to accept what comes to one's end,
but with foresight
there are masses of choices
where enemies can work to become friends!

But to think of a Harris or a Clebold
means to wonder about life as a mystery
or to think of a Jones or a Shouls
means to ponder so much about history!

(June 11, 1999)

Upon Your Birth

We tried to use technology
to see what you would be,
but it was not in the cards
for us to peek and see!

So we waited until your birth
and moved past complications
to prepare your acceptance
on this earth
and strengthen our family's relations!

Who knows if you were born
on the date of someone great
or whether you will be inspired
by unknown challenges you must take!

Whatever your destiny holds
or the sacrifices you must make,
there's no doubt
that yours shall be
a life that's truly great!

(January 31, 2000)

The Ultimate of All Providers

When entrapped by some other
who has devised some great misdeed
and hung a net
over some bottomless pit
for another to fall in and bleed!

If not blood from one's flesh
or some bruise to the very bone,
maybe, instead, a bleeding spirit
whose true innocence is now gone!

No matter what the circumstance
or who might be the great divider,
one can turn
to the truest of sources
that is the ultimate
of all providers!

(December 10, 1998)

52

Sorry for the Delay
(Prayer against Warfare)

Sorry for the delay,
but the devil got busier
so I stopped to pray!

The time was well spent
though it seemed to go on;
with prayers of supplication
time can seem so long!

Continue to pray for me
that I'll do God's will
in this warfare against the devil
where I have to keep still!

(March 31, 1999)

When a Dark Cloud Gets Darker

When a dark cloud gets darker,
there's a sense of urgency
that something awful is threatening
the atmosphere's tranquility!

When a dark cloud gets darker,
there's a need for strong security
that decreases any fearing doubts
about any shelter's durability!

When a dark cloud gets darker,
many things become affected
by the known and unknown outcomes
of the detriments
that might be projected!

When a dark cloud gets darker,
one of the best things to do
is to steal away to some quiet place
and let the true Source
guide you through!

(December 10, 1998)

54

Mustard-Seed Rewards

To survive levels of intrusion,
as we are in the age of such
where simple virtues and values
are conditioned to not mean as much!

But with mustard-seed
faith and submission
as ingredients in all that we do,
there's no situation
we'll ever encounter
that God will not bring us through!

Just remember that the time is at hand
when all of us shall give an account
for the deeds that we have done
for our rewards in equal amounts!

(January 26, 1999)

Judgments of Worth

Judgments of human worth
are made each and every day
through measures of estimation
by our deeds and words we say!

But in truth we seem confined
to consequences of the justified
who uphold a code of ethics
that appear proven
and are more often tried!

Overcoming the depths of judgments
means looking beyond all things seen
to appreciate absolute beliefs
in understanding what others may mean!

(1998)

Transaction Benders

Many things are just a transaction
where there's always something to spend
and the rules are hard and consistent
with little or not room to bend

Because when results don't always equal,
a transaction must have taken place
and some form of compromise is required
to reverse things with orders of grace!

(December, 1999)

To Heal a Broken Spirit

To heal a broken spirit
is to create a work of art
with higher level skills involved
to weave patience into the heart!

Skill and patience are elements
that demonstrates one's ability
to realize what's needed
for a sculptor
supported by facility!

Facility is a matter of tasks
performed in a number of ways
where the heart is truly guided
by spirits the soul uses to say!

Overcome! Move on!
Pay attention to this!

Accept! Reject!
This choice! You can't miss!

So healing a broken spirit
is rewarding when realized
that rewarding efforts achieves
what a true heart can visualize!

(1998)

Foundations for Building

When the builder plans to build,
the foundation is given consideration
because it is a critical factor
in the finished product's substantiation!

Since charity still starts at home
and from there it spreads abroad,
I am reminded
of what grandmother told me
to live and let live
and never defraud!

(1999)

Spirited Souls Are Free

On this site
many years ago
stood an old slave market
and don't you know

That the spirits of those
both enslaved and free
resonate across time
throughout history!

Giving essence to experience
as simple as can be
with proclamations and resolutions
declaring enslaved and free, Free!

Free! Free! Free!

Spirited souls that are free!

Free! Free! Free!

(December 5, 1998)

Instruments of Productivity

I found a needle and thread
in the street by the
once slave market—
historical marker sign!

And the ironies
of this simple discovery
just simply blew my mind!

I thought to myself
how interesting
such incidents
in time and space!

How two instruments
of productivity could meet
at the same time and place!

(September 6, 1999)

Time Belongs

Who does time belong to?
Is it me or is it you?

No one really knows
but one thing is true!

No matter who time belongs to,
we can all truly say
we have the same amount of time
to do great things each day!

(April 24, 1998)

Behavior Can Be Improved

Behavior can improve for everyone;
the job is yours and mine
The task can certainly be done,
but we must take the time!

So much depends on behavior;
it controls the things we do.
We all have to realize
it's up to me and you!

(1998)

Pleading True to the Games

To plead true to the games people play
appears to be the thing to do.
What is not always realized
is that the joke may end up on you!

Those who may call themselves
your friends
may really not be
when things come to an end!

So don't plead true
to the games people play
and if you can beat them
in what they do and say
go on and end things
in a positive way!

And think before you ever plead true—
plead true to the games people play!

(1998)

Test Time Is Stress Time

Test time is stress time;
I need to relax my tired mind.
Some things I say, some things I do
are not kind to me or kind to you;
That's why I know I need to be
considerate of you
and considerate of me
because test time is stress time!

(April 18, 1998)

Thugs

Do thugs really think?
Do thugs even blink?
If thugs were so good,
then thugs would:

Stop the violence;
stop the killing;
help other people;
and be more willing
to save themselves
by being more giving!

Do thugs really think?

(April 18, 1998)

Did You Ever Want To?

Did you ever want to build a sand castle
along the beach's shore?
That span for endless shorelines-miles
that are now, regrettably, no more!

Did you ever want some simple space
or a place where things could be
placed in a haven with solutions
to the great problems from society?

(1999)

Picking Up My Shade

A strong wind and hard rain
blew and fell just the other day
and in its most awesome process
took something so dear away!

There were some weak limbs
on those trees that I love;
They fell to the ground in pieces!

But beside the weak limbs
were green branches and leaves
that meant so much to all of the trees!

I am somewhat sad about my task
as I rake and "pick up my shade,"
but each pile that I pick up
gives the green grass
a chance for blades!

(October 4, 1998)

I Once Befriended a Tree

I once befriended a tree
that made an informal agreement with me!

The agreement was simply this:

I barely survived a fire
where the building burned next to me
and now that it's time for leaves,
I don't feel much like a tree!

Please give me a lot of water
in extra amounts you see
so my leaves can blossom on time
and at least make me look
like a tree!

I agreed to the request for water
in extra amounts you see
so that I could do my part
to help this tree
to feel like a tree!

I even went one step further
and pruned the tree's wild limbs
so it could fill out with luster
and stand out because it was trimmed!

When others pass by and see
this outstanding and beautiful tree,
I take a moment to tell them the story
about the agreement
between this tree and me!

(November 5, 1998)

It's Not the World But the People in It

So many things are blamed
on the state of our world today
and little attention given
to the roles that humans play!

As time and tide continues,
humans still make no resolve
to solve inevitable problems
the human race
will ultimately absolve!

(1999)

People Really Do Matter!

We all need help
in our times of trouble
Even though our shares
seem to more than double!

That is the true importance
of a true friend or good neighbor
Who recognizes the value
of another's diligent labor!

So to be a servant of humanity
is to heed a special call
Where people really do matter
and are important above all!

(On Behalf of True Friends & Good Neighbors)

(June 25, 1999)

People Are Like Pillars

People are like pillars to each other
holding precious time in their care;
they are sometimes like burden-bearers
who toil with more than their share!

Many people are really as kind
as any real or true people can be
by their desire to make simple differences
where difference is all that some see!

So in all that we strive to do,
one thing should always come to mind:
that's the impact of caring and sharing
where the pillars of people are kind!

(January 19, 1999)

To Think About Community

To think about the word community
brings many things to one's mind;
As Webster attempts to explain it
there's one thing that's not defined!

This could be thought of as an element
integrated in a most balanced design
where the interests of all communities
are not limited to borders and lines!

Instead, the bonds of all communities
should be recognized from shore to shore
as efforts increase
towards efforts for peace
with tranquility as hope;
and war, no more!

So we all must have visions of community
that can spread
as all people join hands
building the world
as one big community
respecting the gifts
of the promised lands!

(October 6, 1998)

To Invest in Another's Downfall

To invest in another's teardown
is to place so very much on the line
Making a way for one's own demise
that is only a matter of time!

To invest in another's heartaches
is to assure for one's own true self
The same or some similar fate
that will be yours and nobody else!

To invest in another's downfall
is to risk losses that could be great
Because the integrity
of one's own values
lies in the balance
of what is at stake!

(December 20, 1998)

Pages of History

To write the pages of history
means recording and reflecting the view
Of how things are or ought to be
or change for me and for you!

And when one does that exclusively
the reception may or may not be
In the interest of the good of those
who respect the pages of history!

So be conscious of how you view things
when you record or simply reflect
So that the interest
and good of all concerned
will not end up in abuse or neglect!

As for how the reception should be
keep one thing in mind and you'll see
The genuineness of your descriptions
recorded in the interests of history!

(December 11, 1998)

To Incriminate the People

To incriminate the people
is to subject them one and all
to society-imposed doctrines
that upholds the people's fall!

To incriminate the people
is to mandate a general decline
whereby the progress to be made
is limited to a very fine line!

To incriminate the people
is to burden them beyond all reason
With impositions and intrusions
that go in and out of the seasons.

To incriminate the people
is to have a very strong hand
In the general demise of hope
that will spread across the land!

So please don't incriminate the people;
they all deserve to be free
to stand with the gifts of freedom
with self-respect and dignity!

(October 21, 1998)

To Inspire True Democratic Ideals

To inspire true democratic ideals
is to grasp the unlimited history
that will abound itself to chosen ones
who help to keep their fellowmen free!

To envision true democratic ideals
requires a perception that few can ever see
and an innate ability to translate
envisioned principles into reality!

To progress with true democratic ideals
is to know and to better understand
that the wills of the masses of people
are influenced by an unyielding hand!

So always inspire true democratic ideals
and know wherever it is that you may go
that the contributions
made to the good of others
will reach farther than one could ever know!

(December 20, 1998)

Everyday Frustrations—Simplified in Prayer

*Everyday frustrations
must be simplified in prayer
and made less of a burden
that is fashioned to God's care!*

*The burdens must be given
to a much mightier hand
so that all that remains
are footprints on the sand!*

*The frustrations must not drive us
to those extreme points beyond
some belief that God does not hear us
or simply will not respond!*

*Because our faith must keep us near Him
and be our constant guide
while we lift our hands to heaven
and in God's peace forever abide!*

(January 26, 1999)

A Virtuous Woman

There once was a virtuous woman
who had much favor with God
evidenced by a divine covenance
and an innocence
for the roads that she trod!

Guarded should be one's thoughts about her
as few shall ever attain such a place,
giving voices a spiritual say so
while helping to save the human's race!

We are aware
that reaping time has shortened
and deeds done in darkness
will come to light,
Like the source of one's true convictions
in understanding the wrong and the right!

(January 23, 1998)

Resting in the Loving Arms of Jesus
(In Memory of Nicholas Hallman)

The troubles of this old world
places burdens upon my feet
and passes on to me each day
obligations I cannot meet!

The more I try, the harder it seems
that all efforts are lost to tries
as each day comes and goes
leaving tears of grief in my eyes!

So I'll just rest my eternal soul
in the loving arms of Jesus
and grant to you no tears of sorrow
where things don't always please us!

For God is a God of no mistakes
with all that He has to do
and no matter what the situation
He'll always bring you through!

So while resting
in the loving arms of Jesus,
please don't cry for me,
for I am now in the best of places
that any soul would want to be!

(October 7, 1999)

Criticizing Teachers

There is so much criticism
of those who are called teachers;
why not send them angels
and then criticize them like preachers!

It really would be very simple
if every situation worked out great
where all the finished products
came and went with no mistakes!

Then the tasks of true teaching
would be better understood
and every good intention
would be met with brotherhood!

So don't always criticize the teachers
when so much must be done
with so little
as the tasks of
salvaging futures is done
with broken parts that are so brittle!

(July 27, 1999)

Are Teachers Really Born or Made?

Many have posed the question:
are teachers really born or made?
The answer is really not either
because a self-sacrifice "bill"
must be paid!

The "bill" has various ways to be paid;
it's a matter of a sizable investment
into the depths of inspiration involved
in helping others
to stand as a testament!

So the key is not really "born" or "made,"
the key is rooted
in one's own inspirations
and a committed desire
to be a contributor
to the good of this democratic nation!

(July 4, 1999)

Blueprint for a Good Life

The blueprint for a good life
has simple steps to guide you.
It's not difficult or complex
for determination to get you through!

The blueprint for a good life
can guide you to very good ends
where your hopes and aspirations
become resources and very good friends!

The blueprint for a good life
will extend beyond all limitations,
giving rise to great accomplishments
for the mastery of many situations!

The blueprint for a good life
will not always be popular to follow,
but the satisfaction from having done so
will not leave the heart with a hollow!

(November 5, 1998)

Destimated and Know It

I know I have been destimated;
it was carried to an extreme
whereby all of my hopes and aspirations
were made to not seem
what they had seemed!

I know I have been destimated;
the result is here every day.
It comes to me in hints and signs
that appear just to say:

You! You! You!
or He! He! He!

Did this or that today!

And, oh! By the way!
You're no longer needed here
and here you cannot stay!

So I know I have been destimated;
my self-esteem was shot way down.
But now I have a better view of things
from way down here on the ground!

(October 21, 1998)

To Earn One's Own True Freedom

I recall a continuous vision
of earning one's own true freedom
and rise above the barriers and limits
that entraps the soul's dimensions!

I recall a continuous vision
where one's own true freedom could be spent
being graciously gratefully
for sheer motivation
to triumph over the obstacles that are meant!

I recall a continuous vision
to earn one's freedom and then be
a bounty for spiritual bonds of peace
that will save the world's humanity!

(October 21, 1998)

Am I Human or Animal?

Am I human or animal?
That is the question, you see!
Or am I something other
than who or what I should be?

Am I human or animal?
It's no longer simple for me
since I've resorted to tactics
that stripped my dignity.

Am I human or animal?
I wish that I could see
that other something else
that I'm supposed to be!

Am I human or animal?
I really wish I knew
since this will help determine
the way I treat me and you!

(December 9, 1998)

Life's Sentence to Nine Numbers

I am serving a life's sentence
to nine numbers I did not choose
but by virtue of some mandate
that society decided to use!

It has to do with identification
as it was once explained to me
and it's considered more than justified
under the principles of liberty!

Disregard impositions or simple privacy
and let nine numbers reign
from here to eternity!

And when all is said and done
and the truth may finally be told
of how nine numbers for every person
finally took its toll!

And when all that remains
is a belief to one's self be true
it will be then that people realize
their life's sentence
to nine numbers too!

(October 21, 1998)